T0095300

Nuns

Nuns

Written and Illustrated

by

Jon Buechel

With

Shirley Buechel

iUniverse, Inc.
Bloomington

Nuns

Copyright © 2005, 2012 by Written and Illustrated by Jon Buechel with Shirley Buechel

All rights reserved. No part of this book may be used or reproduced by any means, graphic, electronic, or mechanical, including photocopying, recording, taping or by any information storage retrieval system without the written permission of the publisher except in the case of brief quotations embodied in critical articles and reviews.

iUniverse books may be ordered through booksellers or by contacting:

iUniverse
1663 Liberty Drive
Bloomington, IN 47403
www.iuniverse.com
1-800-Authors (1-800-288-4677)

Because of the dynamic nature of the Internet, any web addresses or links contained in this book may have changed since publication and may no longer be valid. The views expressed in this work are solely those of the author and do not necessarily reflect the views of the publisher, and the publisher hereby disclaims any responsibility for them.

Any people depicted in stock imagery provided by Thinkstock are models, and such images are being used for illustrative purposes only.

Certain stock imagery © Thinkstock.

ISBN: 978-1-4697-7519-7 (sc)
ISBN: 978-1-4697-7520-3 (e)

Printed in the United States of America

iUniverse rev. date: 2/14/2012

This book is dedicated to Jon, my cherished husband
Loving Father of Claudia, Melissa and Bridgit
Adored Grandfather of Paul and Alexandria

We will always love you.

Your loving wife, Shirley

Our world was left a better place because of Jon Buechel.

For 85 years, 10 months and 5 days, our earth was graced by his presence. Anyone that had the pleasure of meeting him once or knowing him for a lifetime can attest that he was a very kind and humble soul.

He left a memorable legacy with his beautiful art, in the fashion world and especially for his weekly contributions to the Detroit Free Press sweetly remembered as "Buechel's World" which captured our hearts and everyday life through the innocent eyes of children.

He also contributed his beautiful art to many charitable organizations over the years, including illustrating annual Christmas cards.

Jon wrote and illustrated "Nuns" a few years back and always had the vision and the dream of having it published. Now with the help of his loving wife, Shirley, she's making that dream come true.

Other books illustrated
By
Jon Buechel

Buechel's World
Whoop for Joy
Laddie of the Light
Lllama on the Lam
The Pretorius Stories

"Nuns"
(A Preface)
Jon Buechel

This book, its humble words and illustrations are done in fond memory and admiration for all nuns, especially the Dominican Order of Racine, Wisconsin.

The dedicated women of God taught me grade school through graduation at St. Clements in Center Line, Michigan, their convent and my home, just a weed field away.

I recall all of their names, manners, the way they taught, even the rooms they taught me in.

Many have left us now, but at a time when their orders and dress have rather disappeared,

These remembrances remain a joy!

2

When the world seemed small
And my years were young
There was nothing
So magical as a nun.

They were my neighbors
Just a weed field away
Fulfilling God's wishes
In the simplest way.

I watched them plod
Their penguin way
To Holy Mass
And school each day.

Through snow or rain
Or sunshine bright
A humble parade
Of black and white.

The convent kitchen
Smelled of pies and bread
And various folks
Were always fed.

I often lingered
Just to see
What little treat
Today's would be?

All strays were welcomed
At the door
A single handout
Never more.

Nuns always walked
In pairs of two
One looked happy
The other blue.

I'm sure they shared
Some laughs, some tears
Their growing up
Their convent years.

Each Monday's wash
Was starched and bright
But now and then
A different sight!

Cleanliness is next to Godliness
So it is often said
In sunshine or in overcast
Bright wash hung overhead.

Some sisters were short
And others tall
Skinny ones, heavy ones
God loved them all.

When gathered together
To work in His Name
God showed no preference
All were the same.

14

One nun was an artist
Another a poet
Another a farm girl
Convent gardens would show it.

They excelled in each gift
Given by Him up above
Tasks, day after day
Performed with great love.

Summer evenings on convent porch
Were spent as one desired
To talk or sew, to read or laugh
Or just get plain 'ole tired.

A sun sets on their busy day
A first star appears above
A time of peace, a quiet time
All given by His love.

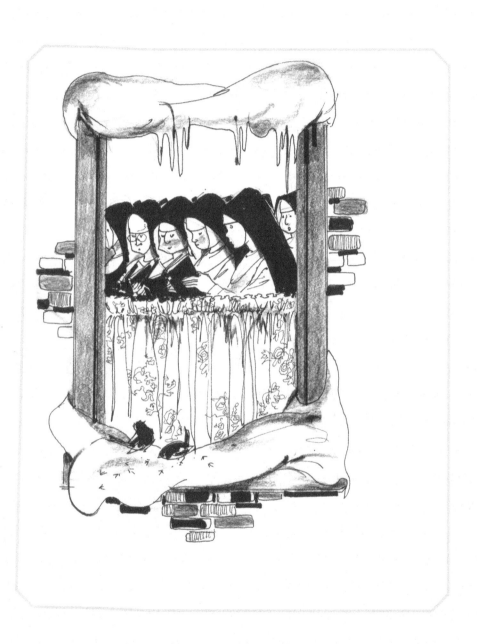

Out on the playground
Like 'ole mother hen
She counts all her brood
Then counts them again.

Their teacher, protectress
Ready on call
Soothe feelings, heal bruises
Guardian angel to all.

The convent chapel
Was a most peaceful place
All windows tiered
With pristine lace.

Hymns were sung in praise of Him
Each note in solemn pace
A metronome of thought and praise
I never can erase.

I often sat
On chapel sill
Where Gregorian chant
The air would fill.

Songs of Benediction
To His love
A heavenly choir
From above.

To this day, I embrace this chant
A gentle rise and fall
An ethereal blessing sung by nuns
A memory for us all.

No chore too demanding
Nor none too little
And one little nun
Could play the fiddle.

Each had their tasks
On certain days
All handled perfectly
In nunnery ways.

Like little children
All aglow
They loved to frolic
In winter's snow.

Some built a snowman
Others tried the ice
Escaping to their childhood
Was Happy, Joyous, Nice!

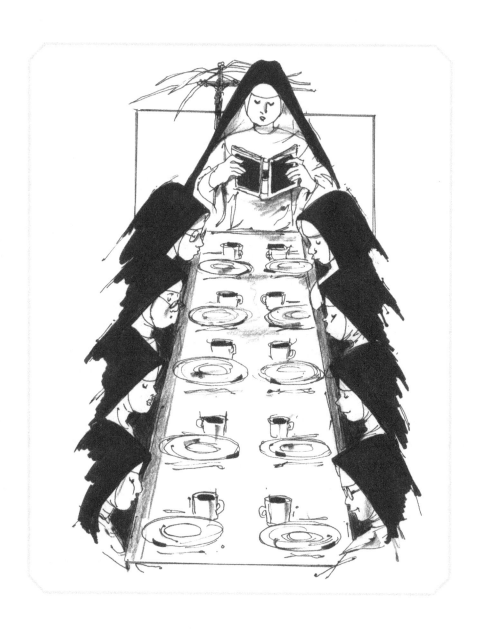

When meals were served
Each nun in place
One sister elect
Would say the grace.

Their thankful time
Three times each day
"Bless Us, O Lord
To Thee We Pray".

Several times
They held retreat
A time for God
And aching feet.

First came time of Advent
Lent, six Sundays in a row
Lay aside the works of darkness
The armor of their God to show.

Now it's Easter Sunday
Christ has Risen from the Dead
Rejoice and Alleluia
Receive the unleavened bread.

In their vows
All took Mary's name
Mary Agnes, Mary Martha
And Germaine.

Sister M. Thomas
Raphael and Rose
Cecilia, Bernard
And Mary Ambrose.

Sister Mary Martin
Vincent, Theresa and Paul
Heavenly patrons
God's saints one and all.

Small gifts from home for each good nun
Brought memories flooding back
Homemade dolls and coloring books
Toy trains around the track.

A star above a humble stable
In straw the Baby lies
A Holy Day remembered
When angels filled the sky.

With aprons on
And pinned up sleeves
They cleaned God's house
Their Lord to please.

Polish, wax
Scrub and dust
Flowers, candles
A Sunday must.

The altar boys wore cassocks
Colors red or black
All tagged with servers name
Hung neatly on a rack.

Pure white surplices
Were organized by row
Sent home to many mothers
To wash and often sew.

Good Sister Madeline
Was in charge of all
To serve this way
Her special call.

Sundays, weekdays
Holy Days and such
All held great meaning
And Sister's special touch.

There were always some cut-ups
She would handle with ease
All of this pageantry
The Lord just to please.

One of the nuns
Just loved to sing
Therefore all music
Was her thing.

She kept her pitch pipe
Ever near
Choir voices heard
Loud and clear.

Hymns of praise and songs of love
Were taught each and every day
Notes flew up and down the scale
All in her happy way.

I always observed
One thing with each
A handkerchief
In easy reach.

Always tucked
In habits sleeve
To wipe an eye
Or catch a sneeze.

An easy place to store a note
Some safety pins and such
To warm her hands on winter days
Her scapular to touch.

The Dominican Order
All from Racine
Had three separate steps
To complete their dream.

First a Postulant
A Novice then Nun
Becoming brides
Of God's only Son.

They dedicate their years to God
To sacrifice and teach
Living lives so humbly now
The heaven's gates to reach.

Their room
A cubical-small, but neat
Their curtained place
In which to sleep.

A tiny lamp, a chair
A desk on which to write
Upon the wall a crucifix
To guard her through the night.

Through Winter
Summer, Spring and Fall
I cherish memories
Of them all.

The younger nuns and older too
Rejoice in each new day
Finding things God gives to each
In His own special way

These humble women
Will always be
Stepping through
My memory.

Teaching us throughout each year
The day would come and go
Soon it came a time to leave
Their caring years to know.

I often create a personal space
A time that feeds my soul
Where all these nuns drift in and out
God's soldiers in a row.

These saintly women
Will always be
A part of my years
And fond memory.

Many have gone now
To their heavenly rest
But while they were with us
They were God's Best.

This book would be of interest to all people who looked forward to and miss the drawings of "Buechel's World".

"Nuns" gives a humorous view of a young boy's remembrances of his neighbors, the Dominican Order of Nuns. Watching the nuns as they lived the human lifestyle of doing laundry, baking pies and bread, feeding neighborhood strays, frolicking in the snow and watching them plod each day in their penguin way to Holy Mass and school.

Biography
Of
Jon Buechel

From little on, "I drew". Seems I was always with pad and pencil fascinated with crayons and paint box and what they could create.

As I grew, so did my interest in line, form, color and texture and I found it all in fashion art. Sketching fashion all those years led to my doing children's clothes and eventually to my kids art and "Buechel's World". One can't go wrong with children and animals. They appeal to all ages.

The happiness and memories and joy of being children are wonderful to express and remain a great part of my paint and brush. Nothing ever wipes out the "abundance" found in kids – all the delight in any situation. There will always be the little ones.

I've been told that my Buechel's World art has hung on many refrigerator doors, that teachers use my art to decorate their classrooms, art that sweet little grandmothers clipped and saved.

When I'm asked to sign my art I most often use the word "happiness". That is what I feel in my art.